I0866887

VALUE BIOGRAPHIES

DETERMINATION
The Story of THOMAS EDISON

KENG XIONG

childsworld.com

The Child's World
childsworld.com

Published by The Child's World®
800-599-READ • www.childsworld.com

Copyright © 2026 by The Child's World®
All rights reserved. No part of this book may be reproduced or utilized in any form or by any means without written permission from the publisher.

Photography Credits
Photographs ©: Library of Congress, cover, 1, 6, 7, 8, 13 (top left), 14, 19 (top); The Henry Ford, 5, 13 (middle right); National Park Service, 9, 10, 13 (top right), 13 (bottom left), 15, 20; Bettmann/Getty Images, 13 (bottom right), 17; Nattawit Khomsanit/Shutterstock Images, 18; Shutterstock Images, 19 (bottom); Design element from Library of Congress

ISBN Information
9781503871212 (Reinforced Library Binding)
9781503872561 (Portable Document Format)
9781503873803 (Online Multi-user eBook)
9781503875043 (Electronic Publication)

LCCN 2024950393

Printed in the United States of America

BRINGING THE WORLD TO YOUNG READERS 1968

Keng Xiong is an editorial assistant from Andover, Minnesota. He has a bachelor's degree in English and creative writing. In his free time, he enjoys traveling and going to bookstores.

TABLE OF CONTENTS

CHAPTER 1

A DETERMINED MIND

In 1869, Thomas Edison was excited. He was going to **patent** an invention for the first time. It could record votes electronically. Edison was an inventor. He worked hard to **improve** older ideas. He also made new inventions. He was determined to make his ideas become a reality.

Edison wanted people to use his inventions. He wanted to make life easier. His vote recorder worked well. But the government was not interested in the device. Edison was disappointed. But he did not give up. From then on, he decided to **focus** on making inventions people would use.

Edison's invention was meant to be used by large groups voting on an issue. There was a switch for each voter. The voter would flip the switch to say "yes" or "no." Then the device would count and print the votes.

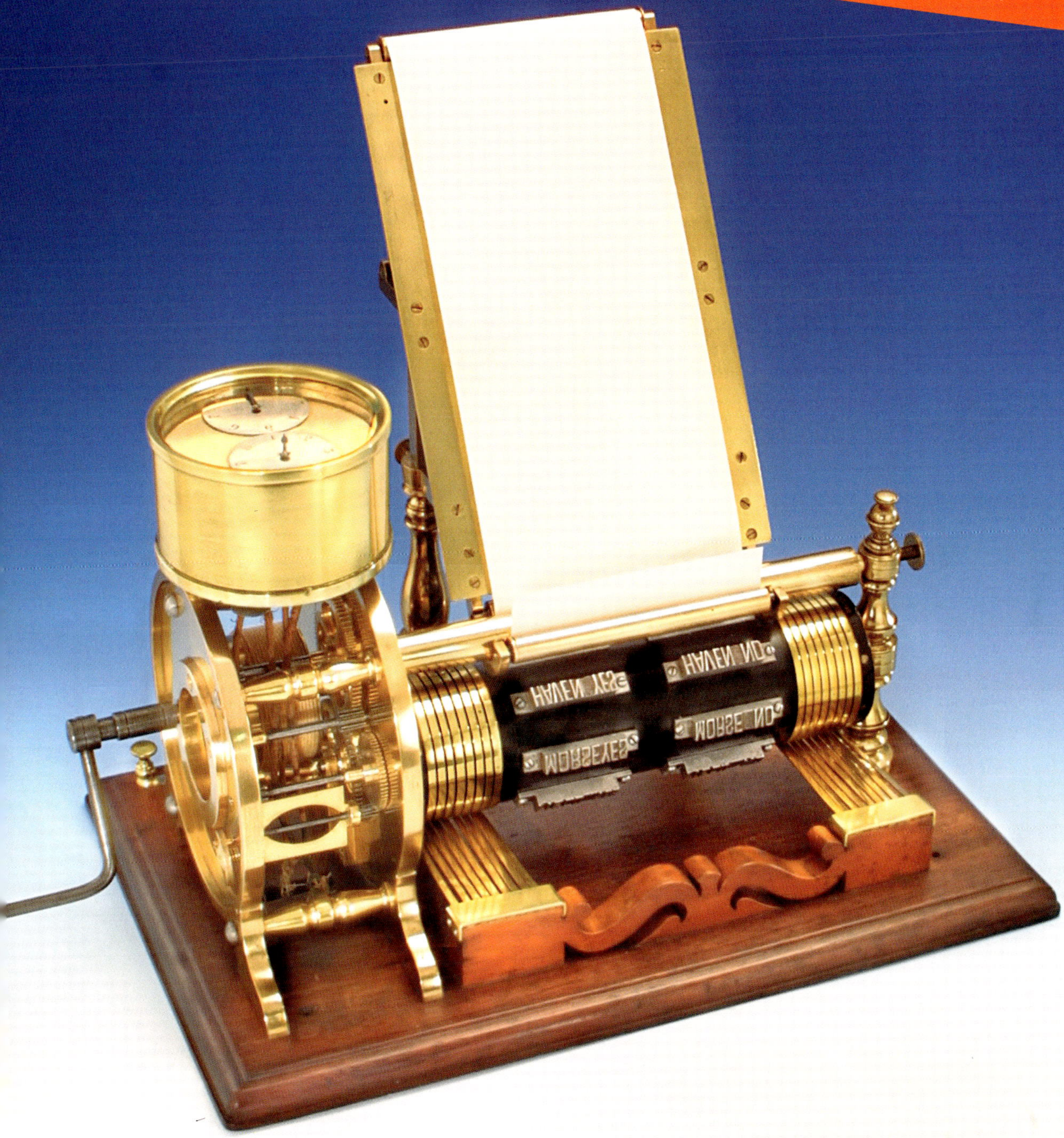

Edison worked with many other people to achieve his goals.

Determination is working hard to achieve a goal. It often means **overcoming** challenges. Goals can be big or small. They can be hard to achieve alone. But people can work together to achieve goals.

Edison showed determination even when his inventions did not go as planned. He asked questions about what did not work. He got help from other inventors. Then he made changes. Sometimes the inventions still did not work. But sometimes they did. No matter what, he was determined to try.

CHAPTER 2

THE VALUE OF DETERMINATION

Thomas Alva Edison was born on February 11, 1847. He was raised by his parents, Samuel and Nancy Edison. He grew up in Milan, Ohio, and Port Huron, Michigan. He was the youngest of seven children.

Edison did not do well in school. He struggled to learn in class. He could not focus like the other students. His teachers made rude comments about him.

Edison around age 14

Edison's mother had been a teacher. She pulled him out of school and taught him at home. This way, he could learn at his own pace. He could focus on subjects that interested him. He learned math, reading, and writing skills. He was always curious. He often studied on his own, too. He grew to enjoy science and doing **experiments**. He was determined to do well. He did not want to disappoint his mother. She motivated him to do better.

Edison opened his Menlo Park laboratory in 1876. In 1887, he moved into a larger laboratory in West Orange, New Jersey.

MENLO PARK, NEW JERSEY

Edison had his own laboratory built in Menlo Park, New Jersey. The place was known as an invention factory. Edison and his workers did many experiments there. They worked long hours to make inventions.

Edison carried this determination throughout his life. In 1862, Edison saved a child from being hit by a train. The child's father was a telegraph operator. To thank Edison, the man taught him to become an operator, too. The telegraph let people send and receive messages over long distances. It sent electric signals through wires. The device made communication easier.

Edison was determined to put his new skills to use. He traveled the country working as an operator. He studied the telegraph. He looked for ways to make it better. In 1868, he got a job at the Western Union office in Boston, Massachusetts. This was a big telegraph company. Being in Boston meant working with major inventors in the telegraph **industry**. Edison worked on telegraph inventions. One was a telegraph that could send two messages at once. He needed to go to New York City to test it. The Western Union headquarters was there.

Edison decided to quit his job as an operator. He wanted to focus on inventing full time.

In 1869, Edison moved to New York City. He began working with Franklin L. Pope. Pope also worked on telegraphs. The two started several businesses together. Edison was thinking of ways to make telegraphs better. He experimented with different ideas. He came up with a telegraph that printed messages on paper. It took many tries, but he eventually succeeded. He continued to work on telegraph inventions throughout his life.

Edison was a talented inventor. But he became known for improving other inventions. Alexander Graham Bell invented the telephone in 1876. In 1877, Edison invented a device that improved the telephone. It created radio waves to make voices sound clearer.

THOMAS EDISON'S LIFE

Edison moved from place to place and created new inventions.

1847 Edison is born on February 11 in Milan, Ohio.

1854 Edison's family moves to Port Huron, Michigan.

1862 Edison learns to become a telegraph operator.

1868 Edison gets a job at the Western Union office in Boston, Massachusetts. He works on telegraph inventions.

1869 Edison moves to New York City to become a full-time inventor. In June, he receives his first patent for an electric vote recorder.

1876 Edison opens a laboratory in Menlo Park, New Jersey.

1877 Edison improves the telephone and invents the phonograph.

1880 Edison patents his incandescent light bulb.

Edison continues inventing. He patents more than 1,000 inventions. He opens and closes several businesses and factories.

1931 Edison dies on October 18.

This work inspired Edison. Telephones helped people talk to each other. But Edison wanted to record sound and play it back. It had never been done before. But Edison was determined to try. He began work on the phonograph. This device would use vibrations and a needle to record and play sound.

Creating the phonograph was not easy. Edison's first idea was to record vibrations on paper coated with wax. This showed Edison his idea would work. Now he needed to bring it to life. A few months later, he created a working phonograph. It used tin foil instead of paper. As a test, he recorded "Mary Had a Little Lamb." The phonograph played back his own voice! Many inventors were amazed.

Edison was **resilient**. He had to believe in himself, even when he faced challenges. He had to think of new ways to go about things. He learned these skills over his many achievements and setbacks.

CHAPTER 3

SPARKING NEW INVENTIONS

Determination means being OK with making mistakes. These failures often lead to answers. They help a person find a way forward.

In the late 1870s, Edison was working on an incandescent light bulb. Incandescent light bulbs use electricity to heat a **filament** inside a glass bulb. It then lights up. Edison needed to find the right filament. This would allow the light bulb to light up for a longer time. Edison first used platinum filament. This worked well. But it was too expensive. He had to think differently. He had to change his goal.

General Electric created a giant light bulb for a celebration of the 50th anniversary of its invention. Edison posed with it, holding a model of his original light bulb.

In 1879, Edison realized carbon worked best. He got carbon by burning materials. He needed to find the right material to carbonize. Edison's first successes used cotton thread and cardboard.

Edison received a patent for his light bulb in January 1880. But he wanted to keep improving. He tested different plant fibers.

Today, tungsten is found in the filaments of incandescent light bulbs. This metal burns longer than plant fibers.

These are threadlike strands that come from plants. He had scientists send fibers from different places. This let Edison and his workers test more materials. They worked together to reach a shared goal.

Eventually, Edison's determination paid off. He found that carbonized bamboo worked best. Edison already had a patent. His light bulb worked. He could have stopped looking for new filaments. But he was determined to make his invention the best it could be.

IN HIS WORDS

In 1893, Charles D. Lanier published an article about Edison. Lanier asked Edison how he came up with ideas. Edison replied:

> *"I never did anything worth doing by accident. . . . No, when I have fully decided that a result is worth getting, I go ahead on it and make trial after trial until it comes."*

Source: Lanier, Charles D. "Two Giants of the Electric Age." *Review of Reviews*, July 1893, p. 44. *Internet Archive*, archive.org.

Edison created many inventions, including the Kinetoscope. This technology allowed people to view motion pictures.

Edison died on October 18, 1931. His impact can still be seen today. His determination led him to improve inventions. His ideas also helped spark new inventions. Edison worked hard to overcome obstacles and achieve his goals. He believed in himself and what he could do. He believed in others, too. He knew when to ask for help. By working together, people can reach even bigger dreams and goals.

WONDER MORE

Wondering About New Information

How much did you know about determination and Thomas Edison before reading this book? What new information did you learn? Write down three new facts that this book taught you. Was the new information surprising? Why or why not?

Wondering How It Matters

What is one way that determination relates to your life? How do you think it relates to other kids' lives? Is there anything you or your friends are determined about?

Wondering Why

Being determined requires believing in yourself. It also means asking for help. Why do you think these things are necessary for determination? Why was determination so important to Edison?

Ways to Keep Wondering

Determination is a complex topic. After reading this book, what questions do you have about determination? What can you do to learn more about being determined?

FAST FACTS

- Determination is working hard to achieve a goal. It often means overcoming challenges.
- Thomas Edison was born on February 11, 1847. He grew up in Milan, Ohio, and Port Huron, Michigan.
- Edison showed determination when working on his different inventions. He worked through many challenges and setbacks. He had the help of others, too.
- Edison died on October 18, 1931. His inventions, such as the phonograph and light bulb, have made a great impact on today's world.

IMPROVING AN INVENTION

1. Edison was determined to improve ideas. Think of a helpful invention that you use in your life. Why is this invention helpful?
2. Now, make improvements to it. What could make this invention even more helpful? What do these changes look like? What materials would you need to make them?
3. Name your new invention and share it with someone. What do they notice about your invention? Do they have feedback?

GLOSSARY

experiments (ek-SPEH-ruh-mintz) Experiments are tests in which a person carries out a series of steps to find a result. Edison did many experiments before perfecting his inventions.

filament (FIH-luh-ment) A filament is a thin, threadlike object. Edison used carbonized bamboo as filament for incandescent light bulbs.

focus (FOH-kuss) To focus is to pay special attention to something. Edison struggled to focus in school.

improve (im-PROOV) To improve something is to make it better. Edison was a talented inventor, but he also worked to improve existing inventions.

industry (IN-duh-stree) An industry is an area of work. When Edison moved to Boston, he met people in the telegraph industry.

overcoming (oh-vur-KUH-ming) Overcoming an obstacle is working to solve it and move past it. Edison showed determination by overcoming obstacles and becoming a successful inventor.

patent (PAT-unt) To patent something is to obtain a patent, an official document that grants someone the right to make an invention. Edison was excited to patent an electric voting machine.

resilient (rih-ZILL-yent) Someone is resilient if they can withstand and come back from a difficult situation. Edison was a resilient inventor.

FIND OUT MORE

In the Library

Henzel, Cynthia Kennedy. *Telephones Then and Now*. Parker, CO: The Child's World, 2025.

Schuh, Mari. *Jada Sticks with It.* Minneapolis, MN: Lerner, 2023.

Xiong, Keng. *Curiosity: The Story of Nikola Tesla*. Parker, CO: The Child's World, 2026.

On the Web

Visit our website for links about determination and Thomas Edison:
childsworld.com/links

Note to Parents, Caregivers, Teachers, and Librarians: We routinely verify our web links to make sure they are safe and active sites. So encourage your readers to check them out!

INDEX